JUL   2004

First American edition published in 2004
by LernerSports

This book is available in two editions:
Library binding by LernerSports
Soft cover by First Avenue Editions
Imprints of Lerner Publishing Group
241 First Avenue North
Minneapolis, MN 55401 U.S.A.

Website address: www.lernerbooks.com

Designed and produced by:
David West ⚊ Children's Books
7 Princeton Court
55 Felsham Road
London, England

Designer: Gary Jeffrey
Editor: James Pickering
Picture Research: Carlotta Cooper

Library of Congress Cataloging-in-Publication Data

Oxlade, Chris.
 Rock climbing/ by Chris Oxlade.—1st American ed.
 p. cm.—(Extreme Sports)
 Includes index.
 Summary: Provides an introduction to the sport of rock climbing, along with information on the sport's history, styles of climbing, equipment, techniques, popular sites for climbing, and some of the dangers.
 ISBN: 0–8225–1240–8 (lib. bdg.)
 ISBN: 0–8225–1190–8 (pbk.)
 1. Rock climbing—Juvenile Literature. [1. Rock climbing.] I. Title. II. Extreme sports (Minneapolis, Minn.)
GV200.2 .O95 2004
796.52'23—dc21   2002013601

PHOTO CREDITS :
Abbreviations: t-top, m-middle, b-bottom, r-right, l-left, c-center.

Front cover - Corbis. 3, 7br, 15t & m, 16r, 17 both, 18, 18-19, 20 both, 26-27, 28t - Buzz Pictures. 4-5, 8-9b, 12l, 14l, 16l, 23tr & bl, 24l, 25t, 30 - Corbis Images. 6t & b, 6-7, 7tr & m, 10b, 11bl, 21, 22-23, 24tr (John Cleare), 8-9t (Bill March), 10t (Chris Craggs), 22, 29l (Ian Smith), 29r (Dave Simmonite) - Mountain Camera Picture Library. 5, 8 both, 9, 11tl & r, 14r, 19, 20-21, 23br, 24br, 25m & b, 27, 28b - Stockshot. 12br - Scarpa / The Mountain Boot Co. Ltd. 13 all - Petzl / Lyon Equipment Ltd.

An explanation of difficult words can be found in the glossary on page 31.

extreme sports

ROCK CLIMBING

Chris Oxlade

LERNER
SPORTS
AN IMPRINT OF LERNER PUBLISHING GROUP

CONTENTS

ACCEPTING THE RISKS
Rock climbing has many risk factors. Most climbers are not foolish. If the risks are too great, they don't climb.

Introduction

Imagine yourself high above the ground on a steep rock face. You climb upward, holding on only by your fingertips and the sticky rubber on your climbing shoes. Even though you are protected by a rope, your brain urges you not to fall. Your arms are tired. But your skill and courage eventually carry you to the top of the rock. Success!

The question climbers are asked most often by nonclimbers is "why do you climb?" For some, it's the thrill of success when they complete a scary climb. For other climbers, it's the physical challenge, a love of the outdoors, or the fun of competition. Every style of climbing has its own unique challenges and rewards.

WARNING!

ROCK CLIMBING CAN BE AN **EXTREMELY DANGEROUS** SPORT. DO NOT TRY ANY FORM OF ROCK CLIMBING WITHOUT **PROFESSIONAL SUPERVISION**.

ADVENTUROUS CLIMBING
Climbers who climb mountains or seacliffs enjoy the adventure. They rely on themselves to avoid trouble.

People have probably climbed rocks for thousands of years. But rock climbing as a sport began only just over a century ago.

The Birth of Rock Climbing

Rock climbing is part of alpinism, or mountain climbing. Alpinism began in the 1800s. It is named after the Alps, a mountain range in Europe. British alpinists began climbing small rock faces in Britain as training for their vacations in the Alps. They enjoyed it so much that the sport of rock climbing was born!

HEMP ROPE
Early climbers used ropes made from a plant called hemp. The ropes often broke when climbers fell!

GIUSTO GERVASUTTI
Italian Giusto Gervasutti scaled many hard routes in the eastern Alps. He died in 1946 rappelling (coming down from a climb).

THE FIRST ROCK CLIMB
One of the first examples of rock climbing for fun took place in 1886. W.P. Haskett-Smith climbed Napes Needle, a rock pillar in England.

ARTIFICIAL CLIMBS

Climbing walls were developed in the 1970s as places to train. Since then they have evolved into impressive structures with rocklike features.

Equipment and Technique

Climbers developed specialized equipment in the 1950s. Rubber-soled boots, nylon ropes, and carabiners (metal links) made climbing much safer. The new gear allowed climbers to try harder routes.

JOE BROWN

Joe Brown was the leading British rock climber of the 1950s and 1960s. He led more than 600 new routes.

BEN MOON

Modern-day climber Ben Moon spends most of his life clinging to boulders.

New Branches

The popularity of rock climbing has grown in the last twenty years. New branches of the sport—such as bouldering and competition climbing—provide new challenges.

Climbing Styles

Rock climbing has several different branches. Each branch has its own thrills and needs different skills. Many climbers try different branches of the sport. Some climbers specialize in just one branch.

AID CLIMBING
An aid climber on a big wall rests on his gear.

Lead Climbing

Most climbs are done in teams. One climber (called the leader) climbs up first. The leader clips the rope through equipment that's attached to the rock. The other climber (called the second or belayer) feeds out the rope. That climber holds the rope tightly in case the leader falls off. This process is called belaying.

LEADER AND BELAYER
The leader relies on the rope and the belayer (the second) to avoid hitting the ground.

Bouldering

Boulderers climb without ropes on boulders or rock edges. They don't usually go more than 15 feet (about 5 meters) off the ground. Any higher could mean serious injury.

THE BOULDERING SCENE
Boulder climbs are normally short and hard. They have two or three very difficult moves. A thick foam mat and another climber "spotting" help to break any fall.

Free and Aid

Most climbing is free climbing. The climber uses hands and feet to hold on and move up the rock. Free climbers use ropes but only to save them if they fall.

The opposite of free climbing is aid climbing. Aid climbers climb up ropes that are already attached to the rock. Aid climbing techniques are used on climbs that would be impossible to free climb.

SOLO CLIMBING

"Soloing" is ropeless climbing on high rock faces. It can have deadly results if anything goes wrong.

ROUTES AND CRACKS

Climbers normally follow a path, or route, up the rock. This route follows a crack.

Lead climbers use ropes and clip them to the rock. The equipment, called protection, protects the leader against long, dangerous falls. There are two forms of lead climbing—traditional and sports.

A RUNNING BELAY
The pieces of protection with the rope clipped through them are called running belays or runners.

Leading a Traditional Route

In traditional (or trad) climbing, the leader places protection equipment into cracks in the rock while climbing. This sort of protection is called leader-placed protection. The second climber takes out the protection as he or she passes it. On some trad routes, there may be few chances for placing protection. These routes can be scary and more dangerous.

ON A TRAD ROUTE
A traditional leader needs experience to decide how often to put in protection and to place it securely.

Leading a Sports Route

In sports climbing, steel rings are already bolted into the rock every few feet. The leader simply clips the rope to each ring. Sports routes (or "bolted" routes) are put up in places where traditional protection is impossible to place.

TRAVELING LIGHT

A sports route requires very little equipment, just a supply of bolt connections, known as quickdraws.

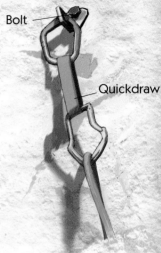

Bolt

Quickdraw

A sports climber clips one end of a quickdraw to the bolt and clips the rope through the other end.

Top and Bottom Roping

In top roping and bottom roping, the climber is protected from falling by a rope leading to a secure anchor at the top of the route. For top roping, the belayer sits at the top of the route. For bottom roping, the belayer stands at the bottom.

PRACTICE MAKES PERFECT

Top roping (right) and bottom roping (left) are used for beginners and for practicing new routes.

Basic Climbing Equipment

Each branch of climbing needs different equipment. Boulderers often use just a pair of rock shoes and a chalk bag. Trad climbers need harnesses, ropes, belay devices, and lots of protection equipment.

Equipment to Wear

You can climb in any clothes, as long as they allow free movement and fit weather conditions. A harness is worn over clothing. Most climbers wear sit harnesses. Very young climbers and aid climbers should wear full body harnesses.

SIT HARNESS

Belay loop

Loops for holding gear

Waistbelt with padding for comfort

Buckles to fasten loops

Leg loops

CHALKING UP

Climbers put powdered chalk on their hands to dry up sweat and to increase grip.

STICKY SHOES

Rock shoes have a rubber sole that gives amazing grip on the steepest rock.

SCARPA

HEAD PROTECTION
A helmet protects the head from falling rocks and during a fall.

KNOW THE ROPES
Standard climbing ropes are 164 feet (50 meters) long. An inner nylon core gives the rope strength. The outer layer protects the core.

Outer Covering

Nylon core

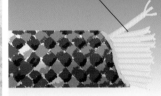

More Gear
Climbing ropes are slightly stretchy. A stretchy rope stops a climber's fall gradually, not suddenly. A carabiner is a strong metal hoop with an opening called a gate.

CARABINERS
This type of carabiner is called a snap-link. Locking carabiners have a mechanism that stops the gate from opening accidentally.

A BELAY DEVICE
A belay device is always attached to a belayer's harness with a locking carabiner.

SLINGS AND QUICKDRAWS
A sling is a loop of strong nylon tape. A quickdraw (or extender) consists of a short sling that joins two snap-link carabiners.

13

Techniques and Holds

Technique is as important as strength when tackling rock faces. Good technique helps a climber to move well and to keep up energy levels.

Feet and Footwork

Beginners tend to climb with their arms, dragging their legs behind them. Experienced climbers know that the secret of good climbing is to keep their weight on their feet. They push upward with their strong leg muscles, rather than pulling up with their arms.

TRUST YOUR FEET
Weight on the feet helps shoes grip holds and steep rock.

KEEPING BALANCE
On steep slabs, staying upright is better than leaning inward. This keeps the weight on the feet. It helps to stop the feet slipping off.

GUIDE #3

BASIC FOOTHOLDS

There are two basic ways of using feet in climbing—edging and smearing.

1. Edging is standing on small ledges with the side of a shoe.

2. Smearing is putting the sole of a shoe against the rock where there is no foothold.

Multipitch Routes

If a route is longer than the length of a rope, it is climbed in sections called pitches. Each pitch ends at a convenient place, such as a ledge. There, the leader ties to the rock and belays up the second.

FALLING OFF
If climbers are about to fall, they push away from the rock to avoid hitting it.

A MULTIPITCH ROUTE
Climbers often take turns leading pitches of a multipitch route.

Traditional Leading

As on a trad route, the leader climbs first to put protection into the rock.

RACKING UP
A climber's protection gear, a rack, is carried on a harness or a shoulder strap

Leader-Placed Protection

On a traditional route, the leader carries the protection gear. He or she brings nuts, hexes, camming devices, and slings. During the climb, the leader looks for cracks and other features where protection equipment will fit. It takes practice to place protection securely, so that the gear will not pull out of the rock if the climber falls. Removing the protection gear is the job of the second climber.

PLACING PROTECTION
A climber tries to find the best spot to place a wired nut.

BUILDING A BELAY
At the top of a pitch, the leader builds a belay by tying onto an anchor (like a rock or a sturdy tree) and then belays the second up.

GUIDE #7
LEADER-PLACED PROTECTION

Camming devices
These have toothed parts that expand to fit in cracks. Pulling the cam makes it jam in more tightly.

Slings
Slings are loops of nylon. They are threaded around rock spikes and jammed boulders.

Nuts
Nuts wedge into small cracks. The rope clips to the wire hoop.

Hexes
Hexes are six-sided metal tubes that jam into cracks.

Getting Down

If climbers can't walk from the top of a climb, they have to rappel. Rappelling is sliding down a rope that's tied to an anchor at the top of a rock face. It may take several rappels to get down a high rock face.

RAPPELLING DOWN

Rappelling is great fun, but be careful not to go too fast or to slide off the end of the rope in midair. Rappelling can be more dangerous than climbing.

You can climb anywhere there's a surface that can be scaled. Popular spots are boulders, old quarries, crags, seacliffs, and rock faces.

SEA STACK CLIMBING

Giant columns of rock, called sea stacks, are a big challenge. The first problem is reaching the base!

Adventure Climbing

More adventurous climbers head for remote mountain crags or towering seacliffs. Falling off isn't the only danger. The rock may be loose. Routes may be hard to follow. The weather may turn bad. Climbers must be prepared to stay out of trouble. Big waves and rising tides are extra hazards on seacliffs.

PROBLEMS

Even the smallest outcrops of rock can offer tough and entertaining bouldering problems.

CLIMBING WALLS
Walls have sections for bouldering, bottom roping, and lead climbing. Walls are popular with beginners. Experienced climbers use them to keep up their strength and endurance between climbs.

CLIMBING INDOORS
Indoor climbing walls are made from flat wooden or fiberglass panels with colored holds.

Big Wall Climbing

Perhaps the most adventurous of all is "big-wall" climbing. Big walls are vertical rock faces often more than 3,000 feet (1,000 meters) high. Routes can take many days to complete. El Capitan is a wall of granite half a mile (one kilometer) high in California's Yosemite Valley. Climbers go up it by free climbing or aid climbing. Climbing El Capitan may take several days to complete.

CALIFORNIA'S BIG WALL
Crispin Waddy relaxes on top of the Texas Flake, more than 1,200 feet (366 meters) up on El Capitan.

World Rock

Luckily, most countries have rocks to climb. Some have more than others! In the last ten years or so, climbers have begun to explore every corner of the world in search of new crags and cliffs.

North America

The United States has the greatest range of climbing of any country. Yosemite offers climbing on smaller crags and boulders. Other popular places are Joshua Tree near Los Angeles, California, and the canyons in the Rockies.

JOSHUA TREE
There are over 4,500 climbing routes within an area of about 100,000 acres at Joshua Tree National Park.

ENGLISH GRITSTONE
Northern England has crags of rough stone, with long cracks and rounded edges.

SUN, SEA, AND CLIMBS IN ASIA
If it's sun and sea you're after, plus great climbing, head for Asia. In Thailand, there are exciting bolted sports routes on dramatic cliffs.

ALPINE ROCK
The Alps offer big climbs in spectacular scenery. There are often glaciers (moving ice masses) to cross to reach the base.

Europe
Britain has a huge variety of mountain crags, low rocky outcrops, and high seacliffs. Most routes are climbed in traditional style. Some cliffs in Britain have hard, technical bolted sports routes. There are huge mountain crags in the Alps. France and Spain are the homes of sports climbing. There, climbers can tackle thousands of bolted routes.

SPANISH ROCK
Spain's Costa Blanca has high-quality sports routes near popular tourist resorts.

AUSTRALIA
Mount Arapiles in Victoria, Australia, has several miles of sandstone cliffs. They make up one of the best crags in the world. The Blue Mountains near Sydney are also a popular sport-climbing spot.

QUITE REMARKABLE
At Remarkable Rocks, South Australia, nature has turned the rock into incredible shapes.

25

Grades, Guides, and Ethics

Every route and boulder that is climbed is given a grade. The grade tells other climbers how hard it is to climb. Different countries have their own grading systems. They also have their own unwritten rules (called ethics).

Grades around the World
Routes are given a grade (and a name) by the first person to climb them. The grade is a measure of the route's difficulty.

WORLD GRADES
This chart compares British, North American, and French grading systems.

BRITAIN (adjectival)	BRITAIN (technical)	USA	FRANCE
MODERATE		5.2	1
DIFFICULT		5.3	2
VERY DIFFICULT		5.4	3
SEVERE	4a	5.5	4
SEVERE	4b	5.6	5
HARD SEVERE	4c	5.7	5
VERY SEVERE	5a	5.8	5+
VERY SEVERE	5a	5.9	5+
HARD VERY SEVERE / EXTREME 1	5b	5.10a	6a
EXTREME 1	5b	5.10b	6a+
EXTREME 2	5c	5.10c	6b
EXTREME 2	5c	5.10d	6b+
EXTREME 2	6a	5.11a	6c
EXTREME 3	6a	5.11b	6c+
EXTREME 4	6a	5.11c	7a
EXTREME 4	6a	5.11d	7a+
EXTREME 5	6b	5.12a	7b
EXTREME 5	6b	5.12b	7b+
EXTREME 6-9	6b	5.12c	7c
EXTREME 6-9	6c	5.12d	7c
EXTREME 6-9	6c	5.13a	7c+
EXTREME 6-9		5.13b	8a / 8a+
EXTREME 6-9	7a	5.13c	8b
EXTREME 6-9	7a	5.13d	8b+
EXTREME 6-9	7b	5.14a	8c

GUIDE BOOKS
Guide books contain names, grades, and descriptions of routes. Photos, diagrams, and maps help climbers find their way around.

Mollywash Wall

99 High Ridge 10m E3 6b   (1976)
The protected bulge right of Guardian crack is climbed
trending diagonally leftwards. A strong approach is needed.
It has been frequently claimed over the last few years and
is therefore known by a multiplicity of names. This is the proper
name, or is it?

100 The Scraper 8m VS 4c   (1958–1964)
A few metres right is a nice jamming crack that slices
a nice little arrete. Well named.

101 Lay Back 6m HS 4a   (1956–1964)
"Layback and think of England" as they say. A well defined
crack leads to a layback below the overhang.

102 Ring my Dell 8m E4 6b   (1986)
Why not climb the right edge of the next buttress. The
bulge above is exciting.

103 Ringu 10m VD   (1958–1963)
Just right are two splits; The left hand one is undercut on
it's base.

104 Ming Peice 10m HVS 6a   (1992)
The skinny face on the right leads to a hard move and a side
runner and on to an easy finish.

105 Ming Climb 11m VD   (1933–1952)
The second crack goes to a platform then on above.

106 Ming's Chimney 7m VD   (1935–1952)
Ascend to the next cleft.

Climbing Ethics

Climbing is a sport without official rules. Different styles of climbing and different countries have their own ethics. Most climbers climb under strict standards. They have to climb a route in one try, and place protection on the way. Climbers can't rest on the rope or practice moves beforehand.

HANGING PRACTICE
Some climbers practice routes on a top rope before leading them.

BOLTING A ROUTE
Bolting is usual in some places. But in others, local climbers want the rock to remain untouched.

Climbing is a naturally competitive sport. There's usually rivalry between friends as they try new routes or boulder problems. Formal climbing competition began in the 1980s on specially built climbing walls.

Three Events

Competition climbing tests a climber's technique, strength, and ability. Three different competition events test difficulty, speed, and bouldering. In the difficulty event, climbers lead a bolted route without seeing it first. In the speed event, climbers race to the top. In the bouldering event, climbers complete as many problems as possible.

BEST IN THE WORLD
The Chamonix World Cup climbing competition is held in France.

BOULDERING EVENT
Competitors in the bouldering event try to complete a series of boulder problems in as few tries as possible.

Amateurs and Pros

You don't have to be an expert climber to enter a competition. Competitions have junior, youth, and adult levels. They start with informal events at local climbing walls. The hardest test is the World Cup. The world's top competition climbers earn a living from prize money and sponsorship (money from promoting brands of equipment).

DIFFICULTY EVENT

An expert climber sets a route by putting bolt-on holds onto the climbing wall. The climber who reaches the highest point on the route wins.

STEEP OVERHANGS

Competition routes are normally on steep overhangs. The holds are small and far apart.

FURTHER READING

Armentrout, David. *Climbing*. Vero Beach, FL: The Rourke Press, 1998.

Brimner, Larry Dane. *Rock Climbing*. New York: Franklin Watts, 1997.

Creasey, Malcolm. *Rock Climbing: Moving up the Grades*. New York: Anness Publishing, 2000.

Hattingh, Garth. *Rock & Wall Climbing*. Mechanicsburg, PA: Stackpole Books, 2000.

Joyce, Gary. *Climbing with Children*. Birmingham, AL: Menasha Ridge Press, 1996.

Lewis, Peter. *Toproping*. Helena, MT: Falcon Press Publishing Co., 1998.

Long, John. *Gym Climb*. Evergreen, CO: Chockstone Press, 1994.

Luebben, Craig. *How to Rappel!* Helena, MT: Falcon Press Publishing Co., 1998.

Roberts, Jeremy. *Rock & Ice Climbing: Top the Tower*. New York: Rosen Central, 2000.

Twight, Mark F. *Extreme Alpinism*. Seattle, WA: The Mountaineers, 1999.

Walker, Kevin. *Learn Rock Climbing in a Weekend*. New York: Alfred A. Knopf, 1992.

WEBSITES

Climbing Online
  <http://www.climbing.com/>
Climbing Tools & Terms
  <http://www.climbing.apollo.lv/frm_e2.htm>
Rock & Ice
  <http://www.rockandice.com/>
Rockclimbing.com
  <http://www.rockclimbing.com/>
RockList.com
  <http://www.rocklist.com/>
The American Alpine Club
  <http://www.americanalpineclub.org/index htm>
The American Safe Climbing Association
  <http://www.safeclimbing.org/>
The National Park Service Park Net
  <http://www.nps.gov/>

All the Internet addresses (URLs) given in this book were valid at the time of going to press. However, due to the dynamic nature of the Internet, some addresses or content may have changed, or sites may have ceased to exist since publication. While the author and publishers regret any inconvenience this may cause readers, no responsibility for any such changes can be accepted by either the author or the publishers.

Glossary

belay: a place on a ledge or the top of a cliff where a climber attaches to the rock so that he or she can safely belay another climber

belayer: a person who controls the rope as a climber climbs, feeding it out and taking it in. If the climber falls, the belayer grips the rope to prevent the climber from falling too far.

bolt: a piece of steel with a ring on the end. It is screwed into the rock face.

bouldering: climbing without ropes close to the ground on large boulders or at the bottom of cliffs

carabiner: an oval or pear-shaped metal ring, used for clipping together other pieces of equipment, such as ropes and nuts

lead climbing: a style of climbing where the climber clips the rope to protection to stop him or her from falling too far

leader: the climber who climbs first and clips the rope into protection

protection: equipment that climbers clip a rope through as they climb. On sports routes, the protection is bolts already in the rock. On traditional routes, it is placed by the climber.

quickdraw: a piece of equipment made up of two carabiners connected with a short nylon sling

rack: a climber's protection gear, carried on a harness or a shoulder strap

running belay (or runner): a bolt or piece of leader-placed protection with the climbing rope clipped through it so that the rope can run up and down

second: the climber who climbs second, belayed from above by the leader. The second removes the rope from protection.

soloing: climbing high routes without using a rope for protection

sports climbing: climbing on routes that are protected by a line of bolts already attached to the rock

traditional (trad) climbing: climbing on routes where there are no pre-attached bolts. In trad climbing, the leader places protection into cracks and clips the rope through it.

Index